Also by Jamie K. Reaser

Winter:
Reflections by Snowlight

Wild Life:
New and Selected Poems

Sacred Reciprocity:
Courting the Beloved in Everyday Life

Note to Self:
Poems for Changing the World
from the Inside Out

Huntley Meadows:
A Naturalist's Journal in Verse

Courting the Wild:
Love Affairs with Reptiles and Amphibians

with Susan Chernak McElroy
Courting the Wild:
Love Affairs with the Land

COMING HOME

Learning to Actively Love this World

JAMIE K. REASER

TALKING WATERS PRESS · Stanardsville, Virginia

Copyright © 2015 Jamie K. Reaser

All Rights Reserved. This book may not be reproduced, in whole or in part, stored in a retrieval system, or transmitted in any form or by any means without permission from the publisher, except by a reviewer, who may quote brief passages.

Front and back cover photos by Jamie K. Reaser
Cover and text design by Jason Kirkey

ISBN 978-0-9968519-0-9
First Edition 2015
Talking Waters Press
Stanardsville, Virginia

"Every day is a journey, and the journey itself is home."
—MATSUO BASHO

MAYBE, THEN

If you can't hear the turkey tail and the bright green
moss singing on the rotted oak corpse, please don't bother me.
If you can't converse with a stone or
haven't even thought about learning the language of birds,
please move on.
Life is short. Each one.
I want my allegiances to be with lovers;
the kind who reach out and invite everything to touch them.
Two hands are not enough for this world
in my humble opinion.
There is so much to hold beyond fear, beyond hatred,
and so we must use our sensibilities to find each other.

Let my prayers be that you will hear the angels at the corpse
and listen for a long while to what the stones know
about the bodies that they have met.
And, the birds, the birds. Let me pray that someday, soon,
you will understand what they are saying about
the need to wake and rise.

Maybe, then, we could take a walk together
and be astonished
by the beauty of this world.
Maybe, then, a poet could be understood.

CONTENTS

COMING HOME TO SELF WORTH
- 3   By Birthright
- 7   Finding My Way Home
- 8   Monarch Butterflies
- 10   Rosie is on the Counter Again
- 11   The Pattern
- 13   A Scarlet Tanager in a Walnut Tree
- 15   Eclipsing
- 17   Part 2
- 20   Listening to the Rain
- 21   Sometimes
- 23   Sunlight Streaming
- 24   The Black Dog
- 25   The Old Tom
- 26   This Drab-Brown Field Cricket
- 27   Boundaries
- 28   My Dirty Windows
- 29   A Moose in the Rain
- 30   Living

COMING HOME TO THE BODY
- 33   Coming Home
- 34   Full Moon
- 35   My List
- 36   Lavender
- 37   Where I Live
- 38   Like An Old Goose
- 39   In the Body of a Woman
- 43   Sunflowers
- 45   Longing
- 47   Meaningful Relationship
- 49   Homecoming

50 A Little Comfort
51 The Annual
53 What the Morning Bird Said
54 Dog Prayers
55 That Which is Enough
56 On Living a Life
56 Consumed by Death

COMING HOME TO THE SACRED OTHER
61 Sisterhood
63 Coming Home to Each Other
65 The Invitation
67 Courageous Vulnerability
69 The Times
71 Praying Mantis
73 In the Morning
74 When it Shows Up
75 Our Home
77 Invitation to the Sacred Masculine
82 Gifting You Roses
83 Fireflies
85 Robins in the Black Gum
86 The Berries
87 Our Friendship
88 Every Evening
89 Morning Rain
90 Short Poem

COMING HOME TO EARTH AND COSMOS
93 Reason Enough
94 Just
95 The Seed
97 The First Sounds of the Morning
99 Caterpillars
101 Nuthatch Logic
102 The Rhythm

105	Who Paints the Sky?
106	Ginseng Thieves
107	The Nature of Cooperation
110	These Bones
113	The Snake
114	You Must Breathe
115	Saying Goodbye
117	Roses Are Out of Season
119	It is Through You
121	The Roots
127	At the Turn of the Day
129	ACKNOWLEDGEMENTS
131	ABOUT THE AUTHOR

COMING HOME
to *Self Worth*

BY BIRTHRIGHT

The tongues that could tell
the story of my childhood
all departed before
reciting it to me.

I've had to listen so very carefully
to my own voice
in order to discern the truth.

Blessings come in this way,

quietly, without fanfare
creeping up on you
all the moments
of your life,

until you realize they
are already there in the council
of day dreams and night prayers,
waiting patiently for your
eyes to be peeled open.

"Good morning, Mary Sunshine!"

Mother used to chortle
as she jerked the bottom of
the white plastic shades,
making them jump and spin
and me bolt upright into
a belief that love is always
coupled with cruel acts
of kindness.

That one has been keeping me
from waking up for a
long time now,

and it could explain why
I never put shades on
my windows,

oddly enough.

Of course there are other
examples,

and I raised myself in
the bouncy infant chair
of all of them.

Growing up has been a process
of severance from
what I never knew,

and a claiming of what has
always been my
inheritance.

We are worthy
by birthright.

Cast-off the hand that attempts
to both slap and sooth,

whether it be yours
or someone else's.

The Beloved speaks only in
verses
that celebrate your
innermost beauty;

it knows from experience
that ugliness

can hide out in popular
places.

Refrain from reading
love letters written
with invisible ink.

Do not dance with someone
who intentionally
steps on your toes.

Admit that you know
when silence is being
used as a weapon

and walk out the proverbial door,
some of you - the real one,
into the presence of
singing birds.

I will make no apologies
for urging you to love yourself
enough to wait in the
vast open spaces of
uncertainty until

the true generosity
of spirit alights
upon your every cell.

No, I will not place
expectations as to the
form in which it
will come.

But it will come.

If you believe,

we are all worthy
by birthright.

FINDING MY WAY HOME

What I have learned:
If you cannot love yourself,
you cannot truly love this
world, with its harsh passions
avowed to setting you free.

The fish on your plate
is a gift from the sea
who asks only for your
salty tears in return;

the air asks only to play
in your lungs.

The swift that you re-member
that you can fly.

I've walked barefoot in mud
in order to find my way
home.

It's the only way I know
how to reconcile my longing for
a mother.

Choose to be.

In the end,

you were the only one really capable
of loving yourSelf
enough.

MONARCH BUTTERFLIES

This is what convinced me of it:

Watching monarch butterflies nectar
on Mexican sunflowers under
a dusty Autumn sky.

How brilliant the orange
of petals and wings!

How I am deeply awed
by these strong, delicate bodies
that float and land,
and support and feed.

How I must ask:

"Really?

These moments are mine to live?"

How they are silent,
yet the world is full of their delight.

How my heart can't contain
this much beauty,

it, simply, can't.

Yes.

I am convinced of it:

We didn't come here to become whole.
We came here to learn how to
break wide open.

ROSIE IS ON THE COUNTER AGAIN

She said to me: "I am important. You should see me." I said: "I do see you. You make it very hard not to see you. You jump on the counters and bat at my face with your right paw." And, she said: "That's not about me. That's about you." Surprised, I inquired: "How so?" And, she circled her lean tortoiseshell body, tail arced, gold-green eyes chasing mine, and meowed, so sweetly: "That's my way of saying: You are important too."

THE PATTERN

There's a pattern to things that emerges
when we stop forcing the elements
into form.

It's the invisible cobblestones
that make up the
circuitous path that lead us
Home.

It's the tempo of the voice that,
one quiet night,
we recognize as our own
perfectly timed
request
to come in.

It's the intersecting lines in the palm
of the hand
that we finally realize
has been leading us where we
never dared
imagine
we could go.

This is what patience means
to me:

Letting life sculpt us
into what Nature
intends.

Like newly dropped
seeds in a some-day
meadow.

Like the clouds
that will become
a pair of dancing
bears.

Like the rain drops
puddling until we
can't resist four-footed
splashing,

and laughing
and hugging.

Let's invite the day to come,

and trust that the night
will follow.

A SCARLET TANAGER IN A WALNUT TREE

Could you for a moment
look up and seek with your
weary eyes
the one singing high in the walnut,

and wonder about him and this passion
he has beating beneath scarlet
feathers – this passion that keeps
him giving voice to
whatever the day is and is going to be?

Are we all born equally this way,
so simply,

beauty?

So simply,
expressions of ourselves?

I think we are.

And, I think this is true too
of the grey squirrel who plants forests
and the rabbit chewing on dandelion leaves at dusk,
and the dandelion being
devoured by a satisfied rabbit.

And, the frog.
Most definitely, the frog.

We needn't try so hard.

Really.

We needn't.

I assure you.

But, who convinced us otherwise,

and why?

This is a big curiosity.

Do you also think about these things?

I, for one, want to be me,

and to consider that
simply,
enough.

I think this is what the world
needs most of me
right now:

To simply be,

enough.

ECLIPSING

"Wear no one's shadow,"
said the Sun,
throwing off the dark
night of the day.

The light you most seek
must be your own,
not a celestial arriving
or re-incarnation of stories
that have outgrown
their telling-time.

These are Earth bound only
to re-mind you of
your own forgotten power
of illumination.

Here.

Here in your vulnerability.
Here in your broken-heartedness.
Here is where you should
look.

Everything that has ever cracked
you open has served its purpose.

All light wants to get out into the world.

When I watch you,

I cannot help but wonder
if the sorrow residing behind
your water-pooled eyes isn't the
cry for help from grieving torch
that you hid
under a belly-scorched bushel
long ago.

You must end this eclipsing of Self.

When?

When will it be alright for you to shine?

I cannot help but think
that the time

is now.

PART 2

So I remained still,
and what found me were ghosts
wanting me to give them names.

Though they had come and lingered before,
they had never asked this of me before,
and it wasn't hard,
it was like remembering the names
of lovers,
or the one name they shared,

and, actually, it was this,
exactly this,

and I was astonished by the profound simplicity
of it.

One ghost,
one name.

And, it wasn't, God.

~

I didn't pay much attention in church growing up.
I scribbled on the yellow-toned donation slips that were tucked into
the back pocket of the pews.
It provided distraction from my father's sobs and
my mother's down-turned face,
and the shame-cast looks of those sitting in front,
behind,
and to the sides.

But that was only for one year.
The ministers didn't want us back after he left.

~

I've been thinking on things, like:

Angler fish
and alligator snapping turtles
and venus fly traps.

In clever ways, they say:

"Come here,
I have something to offer you."

You think it's something good.
Something you want.
Something that will make you feel better,

and all the while they are just hoping
that you are gullible enough
to let them devour you.

It's not personal.
It's just what they do,
and it wouldn't seem reasonable
to apologize for it.

~

And that's when the white dove
returned
to me,

alighted so gently within me.

Firmly.

She is my remembrance of me

as something Holy.

~

That ghost is no longer Holy.

I am.

LISTENING TO THE RAIN

When the rain falls,
steady and long from clouds
resting their thick arms here on
the mountain slope,
I wonder about solitude:
how it teaches you to listen in ways that
prevent you from explaining meaningful things to another soul.
Who wants to be labeled crazy and locked up by
people afraid to have their hearts broken?

What is loneliness?
I don't know.

For now, I belong to this world.
To understand the language of raindrops,
you must first believe yourself worthy
of their kinship.

SOMETIMES

I have learned their language,
some of it,
low scolding screes and chip notes
mean:

"There is a snake in the berry thicket."

I ask:

"What kind of snake?"

And go to take a look.

I determine the species and declare it,
as if they didn't already know or
have their own way with details.
We discuss its length,
and intent.

I'm not sure why we discuss intent. Perhaps,
we believe in surprises but simply need to confirm
that this snake has nothing
of surprise to offer:

It wants to crawl among the bramble canes,
upward, until it can dip its plated head into the
twiggy, leafy, so-much-effort-it-took-to-make-it cup
cradling eggs, maybe nestlings,
and flex its jaws and consume. Empty.

Sometimes I take the snake for a walk,
though I warn that it will return
and I may not be around to hear their calls
the next time. Or, maybe I'll be distracted.

Sometimes I watch what I know will unfold,
unfold. Does this make me a *voyeur of sorts*?
There are days to engage in this practice, I think:

To be there, fully present, with an ending, maybe a death,
without begging or balking, to bring curiosity with you
as an offering of escort to the other world. I can do this.

But, sometimes, I simply turn and walk away, saying:

"I'm going to see if there are butterflies at the coneflowers,"

because, sometimes, I have to remind myself
that there are wild things playing in the sunlight.

SUNLIGHT STREAMING

This morning
the sunlight said things
to me like, "Here. Come
here!" It pointed the way
saying, "Slowly and with
great joy." It went on with,
"There is something around
this bend in the road just
for you." I wanted to
hesitate. I know about changes
in direction. You might have
experienced a few yourself.
But, I kept going. And, the leafy green
trees around me were happy, and the gravel
below my feet was very happy. It made
sounds as I walked. And, there it was!
There around the corner
was the road ahead.
That is all.
The road ahead.
And, for the first time ever, I knew,
without doubt,
that was the road for me
to follow.

And, I took the next step. It was my own.

THE BLACK DOG

The black dog looks at me through big chestnut eyes
and says, "Someone couldn't love me."
And, I stroke his silky ears, and then his soft neck,
and I say, "If they loved you, you wouldn't be
here now, with me."
And, he wags his tail and, I think, smiles
as he exclaims:

"Oh, now I understand!"

THE OLD TOM

Nine years ago, a large-pawed tom sung his way into my small cabin. He's not happy. At sunset he has been taking to the window sill, waiting among the orchids. I watch. And, I wait too, but not so earnestly. Eventually, I get distracted by something else, a chore most likely, and that's when it begins: the growling, the arched posturing against the pane that I should get around to cleaning sometime soon. "He's out there!" he says. "Another one!" And , I turn on the porch light and confirm, "You are correct." A lean brown tabby streaks into the darkness. And, then I say, "Be nice. Don't you remember when you were scared and hungry and alone? It was not so long ago." And, he looks into me with sharp golden eyes, locked. Annoyed, I think. "I'm getting old," he replies. "Our time together is short. I will not share you." And, to make his stance clear, he turns and marks the front door, the threshold of our shared life, our cozy home. Suddenly, I'm back in high school Humanities class, studying mythology. Sooner or later, I recall, the gods always get jealous.

THIS DRAB-BROWN FIELD CRICKET

How many times must a soul vanish into the dark abyss
before it can be known by the body that has been conveying
it across holy ground?

Maybe, at some point, I'll be able
to tell you.

Any heart that has dared be present in this world knows despair.
Despair is what frees us from our attachments to illusion,
what takes us back to that place where the three worlds touch.
Despair whispers, "Now, go forward. Follow this path."

But, you have to love yourself enough
to be able to hear these words.

I've been watching how the ravens fly in tandem
over the hazy blue ridgelines,
and how mushrooms emerge after rains
with little clots of red clay
settled on their heads; evidence that their soft bodies
broke through something hard. And, I've also noticed how
the little native bees with metallic green bodies share
in my love of bold flowers.

It is so easy to find the sacred; simply
stop believing
in the mythos of the profane.

This drab-brown field cricket, ambling her short life
through a maze of dead leaves and dying grasses,
is the next being I shall choose to worship.

BOUNDARIES

These old meadow-larked fields have their
tumbled rock walls with golden lichen suns,
and the forest, its shaggy edge.
My cabin has a magnificent mahogany
door, solid and rich vibrant brown,
salvaged from someone who could not love it
like I can; do not give away privilege to the
first hellos and last goodbyes of any given
day unless there
is great joy in it, and some amount of longing.

Boundaries have their place.

When I first moved to this mountain land, I
raced about in the thick duff putting up

'No Trespassing'

signs on any tree that would agree to hold them.
But the trespassers and those big black bears take
them down: one malicious, one curious.
I've calmed a bit about the lines, well, more
accurately, somewhat surrendered, now making a
mark with silver paint, brushing on my grief for feeling
the need to do this at all – to say "No!" because
the sacred is not always understood on sight.

What does one make of a life like this?
How many marks are needed
and in what form
for a woman to be heard?

"This is threshold of my home."

MY DIRTY WINDOWS

Someday you might visit. So, I need to tell you
this: I keep my windows dirty. I'm not a bad
housekeeper. My mother was. And, she'd say so.

I like the birds and feed them because I've heard
that you should feed the holy, and also because
it makes me happy to see them so delighted.
They are. You can tell. They have their ways of
expression, as I have mine. Though I'll admit, theirs
are much better.

But, sometimes birds see things that aren't there
and make bad choices based on these illusions.
Head first they go, hard, often. The window
pane is not a forest, not the sky, not another set
of feeders full of tidbits to gleefully chip and
fluff about. But when the lighting is just so, they
don't get this. Sadly. No.

Have you ever held one that hit and fell, lifeless?
The spirit goes out of winged ones fast. I suppose
that is because they already know how to fly. Or,
they already know which angels to call by name. Or,
they become angels. These are some possibilities.

So, do you now understand the smears and splotches?

Maybe. Likely not. I say this kindly. I'll explain.

My windows are dirty so that I will remember to be
thoughtful, discerning. I've seen a lot of things in my
life. Some of them, I later found out, weren't what
I believed them to be.

A MOOSE IN THE RAIN

She thinks the face of a moose is as sad
as the face of Jesus. But, Jesus didn't look
sad when we met. And, the moose, he
was, I'd say, fully accepting of his awkwardness.

All my life, I've been trying to be that moose,

though, until now, I wouldn't have said "moose,"
maybe "duckling," because that's the story I
remember being recited to me, repeatedly, during
an awkward childhood; they, perhaps, thinking it
a salve, but I've never looked and seen a swan
looking at me,

so when I saw him there, his fleshy proboscis
lipping shrubbery in the pouring rain of Denali,
his body his own and soaked in its true nature,
I thought:

"This is magnificent! I am a moose."

LIVING

Everything that is me, cannot be
contained in one version of me,
cannot be contained at all,
really. There is so much in here
that wants to get out into the world
and try on a thousand – maybe
a million – ways of being. "What
do you do?" Oh, so many things.
So many wonderful things.

COMING HOME
to the Body

COMING HOME

Good evening,
the blackbird is warbling
a soliloquy
that does nothing
to fill my bed.

Somewhere between now
and there
is a horizon line,
and a day that we could
both call tomorrow.

This feels like the heart
reaching a conclusion –

it can only ascertain
what is right
and what is wrong.

I've read your palm
with my entire body,
and I know what it says.

I am coming home.

FULL MOON

If you are a sensitive soul,
your body is speaking now. Audible
memories rising. Dusk
descending from the mountain,
asking for the quiet
that comes after you've let

it all go, however you do that.

No beauty demands an audience, nor
needs to: Nature has well-organized witnesses.

How many are awaiting her, and what will they
think of this world when she arrives? Is this about faith?
Is it a prayer? If so, what are we praying for tonight?

It could be about peace, as long as the parishioners realize that
peace is not a passive thing. I can't pray for that,
it would be like praying for nothingness
and I want the world to be full.

Two hours more,
while the bright green katydids rub themselves into song
and the screech owl worries the dogs with its tremolo.
I'll wait, if I can, to make my offerings of gratitude:
I'll look up as I've done for lifetimes and
be thankful for each month's opportunity

to become human again.

MY LIST

"How does one live a meaningful life?" I asked this question.

A song sparrow chipped at dusk, three times, and started
me thinking about what it takes to know that out there in the
creeping dark, it is he, Song Sparrow, without a doubt, I hear
giving thanks for the pleasures of the day. So, I made a
list of requirements. I'll read it to you.

1. Notice that you are not alone in the world.
2. Become interested in something besides yourself.
3. Engage in relationship.
4. Learn what makes a good offering.
5. Serve the other in this way.

That's something.

LAVENDER

The bumble bees and I
are drawn to elongated
crowns of lavender flowers
on erect emerald stems.

Only in a world in which
souls can rub up against each other
could you find such creation –

enticing to all the senses.

Let me be here in the physical –

to feel,
to smell,
to see,
to hear,
to taste the knowable,
to intuit the Great Mystery.

Might these alluring blossoms
and these yielding insects
be evidence of our Godliness,

and that every living thing
is a mated aspect
of Heaven?

My body says, "yes."

WHERE I LIVE

"Where are you going?" asked Crow.
"Home," I answered.
"Is that a place?" asked Crow.

"It's like a roost," I said. "And,
a nest. A roost and a nest combined.
Well, it's where humans do most
things," I concluded.

"Oh," he replied. "Then why are you
out here in the woods with us
every day?"

"Because," I answered,

"This is where I live."

LIKE AN OLD GOOSE

I've heard people say in rapid passing, "You must be clever to find the words that describe a day." This astonishes me. Always. Isn't a day simply there, turning about, perhaps like an old goose situating herself on a bed of down, in the gratitude-chamber of your heart?

Nestle deeper.
Be still.
Crack open.

IN THE BODY OF A WOMAN

I've been searching for the
source of your fear –

The wound that you
have forgotten,
but never healed.

The wound that has not
forgotten you.

How can any human being
choose to desecrate the
holy vessel from which they
emerged?

You were conceived
in the body of a woman.

Your father's best swimming sperm
found your mother's luminous egg,
and they joined in union.

You are nature's miracle.

In time, your fingers and toes
took their form in the body
of a woman.

You wiggled them delightfully.
What wonderment.
And sucked your tiny thumb.
What comfort.

You became unmistakably human
in the womb of a woman.

I'm curious:

What about that disgusts you?

Please, tell me. I want to know.

In the body of a woman.

You've burned us,
beat us,
stoned us,
owned us,
molested and raped us –

body and soul.

Witch.

Whore.

Chattel.

Cunt.

Bitch.

Mother.

Daughter.

Sister.

Aunt.

Niece.

Do my breasts actively offend you?

Does my vagina scream profanities?

Do you think my loins are the Devil's hiding place?

Please, help me. I want to understand.

In the body of a woman.

This, my body, is nourishment.

This, my body, is love.

This, my body, is creation.

Why does this, my body, terrify you so?

Please, sit with me awhile. I want to embody compassion.

In the body of a woman.

Wounds are not healed through bloodshed.

Wounds are not healed through oppression.

Wounds are not healed through loss of dignity or shaming.

Wounds are not healed in ink.

Oh why are you compelled to try to do so?

Please, take my hand. I want to help you find another way.

In the body of a woman.

I've been searching for the
source of your fear –

the wound that you
have forgotten,
but never healed.

The wound that has not
forgotten you.

Please, listen for just a moment.

Please, I want you to hear just this:

If I could take your body in my open arms,

and heal all your wounds,

I would.

In the body of a woman.

SUNFLOWERS

There are many kinds in my garden.
I grow them as teachers.

I love them; how they embody joy
in a way I find curious and, on days that
I won't tally,
elusive.

What is it like, I wonder, to be the thing
on which soft bumble bees alight (they are soft,
I have petted them) to collect their dusted gold,
or butterflies – the fritillaries, sachem skippers,
and monarchs – nectar their brave, dazzling lives,
or a differential grasshopper sits long enough to
complete his survey and report unto God
about the things going on down here?
If I chose not to plant them, it wouldn't be such
a happy garden, and this could be one of those
unlived lives that catch your eye at check out.

It's true.

I'll tell you that summer has gone and they – the
sunflowers – are now bent at the waist by
the weight of their heads, looking
like skinny monks at prayer seeking
emptiness
as fulfillment.

This is when I begin to listen most carefully to the soft
om resonating across the beds of straw at their feet.
Hear now, the wisdom gained from two months
of standing still,

and in the last breath of a well-seasoned death
that I record in my cells,

a vow of endless servitude:

"Now, I shall feed the birds."

LONGING

I have been waiting for you so long
that I have taken Longing as my mate,
consecrated in holy union
by the new moon and a great-horned owl
who received her light upon white oak limb.

Dare you come to me in the flesh,
pray you know courting
as the bee knows courting,
buzzing sweetness to his floral love
for the consensual spill
of gold-dust pollen.

Pray you have walked with naked feet
so long upon this Earth
that you know how to caress the feminine
in all her aspects and seasons.

Pray that you long to be received
with a hunger so profound,
and to this day insatiable,
that you know that your only
hope of soulful salvation is
bodily surrender to that which
will devour you.

I pray,
that in the moment of your arrival,
I know you as the
stranger who has long been
my familiar,

the scent after storm,
the voice on the breeze,
the face in the cloud at sunset.

I pray that I know myself
well enough
to stand
and stay
and acquiesce my fears
to a daring do heart.

Longing has been my ritual.

May loving bequest us,
each to the other,
and us in service of the world,
in the language of ceremony.

MEANINGFUL RELATIONSHIP

The dew-dampened swallowtail
braves her first flight of the day,
heavy with night on her wings
but compelled to risk everything
for voices calling out to her to nectar
them into service.

We can't do this alone,
this gifting of ourselves,

this making meaning of our
our embodiment.

Everything is longing for you to give
it purpose through relationship.

Inhale plant.
Exhale animal.
Inhale plant.
Exhale animal…

The ochre-colored grasshopper
half-floating, half-sunk
in the water bucket
showered my hand with dainty kisses
when I lifted him, dripping,
and kept him company in the sun
until he could cast into the
grasses and strum.

Today, it was our task
to love each other.

Tomorrow, the birds will sing
for me as I leave them
an offering of striped
sunflower gratitude.

The toad will wink at me
with his left golden-orb
and puff his heavenly body
when I pass him on the
muddied trail,

saying, "Hello Handsome."

There is no end to the possibilities
of what we could do for each other.

Sit with that for a spell.

~

"How can I help?"

With these four words,
you can live
the meaning of life.

With these four words,

we can make a world.

HOMECOMING

I'm thinking about what happens when you go back
to a place that was once fond of you and see all
those strangers you've known for many years,
and how so much will have changed, undoubtedly,
but not the fact that you are still wondering who you
are and how all of this is supposed to fit together,
somehow. There are bridges that convey us between two
points on this Earth, and others that take us
on entirely different journeys. I've stood on both.
I want to see the ducks, yes, of course, the ducks of
the ducks that once held my confessions, hear the
yellowed beech leaves crackle beneath my boots,
and try, very hard if I must, to remember
things that I never thought were important. Somewhere
along the winding brick pathways and boxwood-edged
gardens, I'll stop and say my hellos to some soul or another.
I'll mean everything I say in the words that follow. A poet
is always earnest. The trouble is though, we never truly
find our way home. And, we know it.

A LITTLE COMFORT

I do believe that there are things out there trying to get us to notice the miraculous. There are choruses at sunrise, and colorful mosaics – like stained glass windows – crafted among the trees at sunset.

They say: "This is a house of worship."

They say: "Listen. Look."

They ask: "What is it that you have been praying for?"

And, I often sit with that question for quite some time. I've prayed for a lot of things, usually not realizing that I was praying at all. Usually, prayers about brokenness – mine or someone else's.

But now, I do choose to pray. Sometimes, silently. Sometimes, through words shared with the world. Never, big. Never, flashy. Often, I just want to bring a little comfort to a soul – mine or someone else's.

A poem can be a prayer.

THE ANNUAL

Your presence would
terrify me
if it weren't my desire
to be destroyed.

I am like the flower
who yearns to drop my
petals so that I may
go to seed,
and bloom anew as
an entire meadow
perfuming the sky.

This self is a limited
concept –

it pushes had against
my inner-skin,
saying,
"Let me out!"

The tight-bodied seed
of me cracks open.

The unfurling sprout of me
rises through the soil,
wishing to speak only
in the plural.

This is how I live –
rooted and
reaching for the sun.

And this is why
I choose to die
an annual —

so that there is more
of me to give myself
to you.

WHAT THE MORNING BIRD SAYS

What happens when a body comes home to itself,
flesh and spirit, shadow and light, recognizing
kinship and the marriage vow that must
be taken in silence to hold true? It is
the animal remembered, a wild being whose
eyes pool with the sad reflection of domesticated things.
It is hands tearing things down because
the feet long to be bare upon sacred ground.

This time tests a soul, hard questions against bruised skin.
What is real? What is your freedom worth?
Do you remember who you agreed to be?
When I was born into this world, I heard a morning bird say:
"You don't belong here, and all your life you will know it.
We are counting on you to help us
find our way home."

DOG PRAYERS

If you are stroking a dog's soft ears,
you are praying for something
better to become of this
world. Perhaps, you don't see my
logic,
but I bet you can
feel it.

THAT WHICH IS ENOUGH

On most days, we move
well beyond the speed of necessity,
adrift in so many wants and not wants –
rushing toward,
running away from.
But there are also days that arrive,
slowly, often by surprise;
here to remind us to stand still,
to be attentive,
to let the world move through us,
to encompass us as if in an embrace
that we remember from somewhere below our skin,
though we're not sure how, or why.
We learn to stay, if only for a moment,
empty of everything
but that which is enough.

ON LIVING A LIFE

"Be without answers at the end of every day.
Start each morning with questions.
Do what you want in the in-between,
but be sure that it gets you muddy,
and wet, and perhaps a bruise just below
your right knee cap. The briars will require
that you mend that hem. If I were you, I'd go
about naming something that you've never
before seen. Then you will be able to call it
and it will come to you and you can have
delightful conversations.

Be sure to introduce yourself first, if you
know your own name,

and, get curious about it. Wonder. To do a good
job, this is a must. And, be polite. Always say
thank you; how this world became so lacking
in gratitude I just do not know. Such simple
gestures could save us all.

On with it, then. You have this life to live,

And, I haven't got all day to sit
here on your window screen."

"What's that?

Oh, you are most welcome."

This happened.

CONSUMED BY DEATH

Sometimes Death leaves us
there, at roadside,
without apology
or explanation.

Stillness resides in nothing
but our form,
all else whizzes past
with agendas.

The palm of my right hand
has known the pulse of the
very last heart beat
beneath feathers and fur,
and skin that I watched wrinkle
for twenty-seven years.

This is my decision:

I don't want to be abandoned
by Death –

I want to be devoured.

I want to be taken into
Death's wet, gnashing mouth
as a wanton carcass,

insatiable in my desire
to surrender.

I want to be consumed
in my entirety,

to be nothing to which
to attach a eulogy to.

I want to depart this world
with less than I brought
into it.

When the last morsel of me
can be described as nothing
more than the last tidbit
swallowed by Death,

then, I will know,

then, I will know,

yes, I will know,

my life had been juicy enough.

COMING HOME
to the Sacred Other

SISTERHOOD

Not by birth, but by vow.

We stand in solidarity,
hands interwoven into
peace-filled fists of unity.

This is sisterhood.

When we cry together,
when we laugh together,
birth miracles together…

This is sisterhood.

Mooning synchronously
and bleeding for each other
from hearts ravaged by
understanding…

This is sisterhood.

Each time we face the mirror,
gazing lovingly into the tired eyes
of every other woman
in the world,

this is most definitely sisterhood.

Sisterhood is what brought
us here –

to this time,

in this place.

We have found each other now,
because we need each other now.

We vowed –

simply

to show up.

COMING HOME TO EACH OTHER

The blossoms are departing
the white dogwood boughs
as the black vultures
hop, hop the grassy bank,
jockeying for position to take
a bite of the doe
who left her body beside Route 33.

In the midst of it all, a sulfur butterfly
lifts himself into the sun-warmed gusts
on untested wings, saying:

"I had no idea!"

A mystic once told me that we
are all inhabiting different
worlds of simultaneous experience.

I'm pretty sure he was right.

And, I think these inner landscapes
we steward must be rich and varied terrain,

though no less bold and fragile,
no less abundant and endangered,
no less invadable and war torn,
no less sacred and celebrated

than the ground we walk on.

It's from here, after all, that we source
our way of walking.

I'm getting used to being lost
in these places –
the inner and the outer,
yours and mine.

I'll readily admit to being mapless.

I have no intention of knowing you completely,
and I'm too great a conundrum
to myself to explain.

I'm convinced this is a good thing:

Mystery is what keeps us longing,
and longing is the power

that calls petals to journey,

vultures to disembark the sky,

and butterflies to risk everything
for a moment of surprise.

How wonderful this dilemma:

We are always in the process of
coming home to each other.

THE INVITATION

I find myself wondering if it's just not being heard.

These things happen every day.

Recently, for me, it's come in the form
of a little red screech owl.

In the afternoon, when the
sun gives just enough warmth to
mask November's chill,

I arrive…

having hiked to the mountain top

…like a parishioner standing
below a pulpit, looking upward
for something that I don't yet know
how to fully believe in,

and he sits there snugged in the three-quarter hollow,
eyes closed, feathers fluffed,
some lifting and twisting at the edges
when the wind's fingers pass by,
others rising and falling…

"Did you see it just happen now?"

…when he breathes.

And that's it.

That's the invitation.

That's the response.

That's our ceremony.

To fail to show up and participate
would be to deny that persistent voice
that is constantly asking me,

"Did you see that miracle?"

COURAGEOUS VULNERABILITY

I want for you
courageous vulnerability.

Please sit for a while and listen
to the ferocious whisperings
of my heart, and yours.

How can it be so frightening
to tenderly touch below this skin,
which cloaks us so temporarily?

I once came face to face with a mystic
who taught me to cascade love
through our eyes
on the wavelength of intent.

It was simultaneously
terrifying
and rapturous.

Nothing has appeared dull since.

I want this for you…

this endless intimate gaze and glint.

I want for you the conviction
of a firm and open stance –

to be a heart warrior
who welcomes the piercing
of Life's blade
at the hands of the Beloved.

May you be met in your bloodletting
by those who
know what it is to
surrender victoriously.

I want this for you.

This, and nothing else,
is the full celebration of
our humanity.

THE TIMES

The men have gathered in council.
Some say that it is time they decide
to remove the knives from the backs of
the women.

There is great fear in this:

"A woman is a powerful thing when whole."

But the sun has decided –
He wants to be sacred again,
and he gives each man enough courage
to risk his head.

These are tenuous times.

The women have gathered in council.
Some say that it is time they decide
to again trust the men to have their backs.

There is great fear in this:

"A man is powerful when seen with integrity."

But the moon has decided –
She wants to be sacred again,
and she gives each woman enough courage
to risk her heart.

These are tenuous times.

Nevertheless,

The day transpires in the form of a miracle,
though ordinary enough to be disguised
as destiny.

[The time is coming]

Tonight each man sleeps soundly,
his head cradled lovingly
in the lap of a woman.

Unknowingly, they had been waiting for this day
for such a long time.

PRAYING MANTIS

All day long the mantis is there,
praying atop the tall purple coneflower,
a vestibule to other worlds

Where wise ones answer:

"It's already been gifted to you,"
and hope we realize this soon enough.

Butterflies come.

Some brilliant and new to air, still
marveling at what has become of them,

Others thin-winged and edge-tattered,
realizing that beauty alone cannot
save a soul.

It's never over quickly.

When the mantis strikes and takes
a great spangled fritillary into her arms,
folding it against itself so that the underwings
reveal iridescent constellations to the heavens
and the long, soft body is easy to taste,
I must resign myself to this.

I must sit with this, this pain and death
that is an
answer to a prayer,
this sound of tiny mantis mouthparts scissoring
into flesh that yet twitches and I believe
knows the agony of form and spirit.

Yes, I must.

Because this is it. Life.

And it must be looked at and sat with
and listened to long enough to realize
that crickets are chirping and crows cawing
and barred owls asking "Who cooks for you?"
and acknowledged that I do this too, every day.

And this is how I remind myself
what it is
to have prayers answered.

This is how I teach my heart gratitude.

IN THE MORNING

Do you know mornings that refuse
to fully release
the night's dreams?

I do.

I've learned to apprentice to them,
their want for me to re-member
that I am alive in other places,

that what we most long for can find
us when we are still.

A small white feather drifted, downward,
falling in gentle swinging motions, coming
from the clear blue sky onto land
that we had stood on together, side by side,
so very long ago,

I could remember the texture of the warm
soil under my bare feet,

and the view of the side-sprawling mountains
on the salty-blue horizon that we had
walked towards with an intent to be
something else,

and I wondered

how the white dove you had gifted me
found me again.

WHEN IT SHOWS UP

When it shows up,
you should go outside and make offerings;
you never know what form a god
will take.

Sometimes it's a wild thing, but more
likely a cat, or a dog,
once it was a sheep, really,
today, a white pigeon
– not a dove –

that I gave seed in my grandmother's
cereal bowl, painted by hand with a fruit decor,
by someone who might now be
someone's angel, or just gone,

I won't claim to know how these
things work, although I do have
my ideas. As, I'm sure you have your own.

Who has lost their way?

Standing on my door step, I often wonder
which one of us

most longs to be found.

OUR HOME

The memory of experiences I've never had
has been passing before my eyes –
unlived lives wanting to be laid
to rest.

It's not sermons they are looking for,
but cascading tears –

the kind of tears brave enough
to tell stories in empty rooms.

When the rain falls hard and long
against the window pane,
the multitude of coalescing droplets
can confound the ability see what
is on the other side.

Only upon reflection is
there faith.

I look to the wildflowers
smartly gracing the
curvaceous vase
on the old scratched dresser.

I wonder: Why do I keep one
element out,
and escort another in?

It's the purring cat that reminds
me that being touched
is an act of relationship.

This, our home, must not be
a fortress,

or a cage.

There is a reason the
skin tingles.

INVITATION TO THE SACRED MASCULINE

I know how long you have
been waiting to be received.

I have heard the desperate cries
from the little-boy-of-you –

The one who wants to be held
in ways he's never
truly been held.

I've felt the pain projected
from the adolescent-of-you –

The one who believes that
you have to test love by
being unkind to the ones
who say they love you.

I've seen the fear,
and sometimes the rage,
in the young-man-of-you –

The one you self-sent to war,
hoping that embattlement
would make you a Hero.

This poem…

This poem,
is an invitation that I'm writing
to the initiated-adult-of-you –

The one who understands that
vulnerability and courage
can reside in the same body,
simultaneously,

And that these are the gateways
to intimate communion
with the Sacred Other.

The one who knows he's tended,
always and forever,
by the Great Mother,

and who has come to his knees
in humble gratitude and
reciprocal offering for the
nourishing milk of Life that he
has received daily from her supple teats.

The one who has learned
the difference between the
ego's encampment of the hero
and the hero's journey of the soul,

And who has chosen to no
longer believe in enemies,

but who actively fosters extended families
of sisters and brothers
among the two-leggeds, four-leggeds,
feathered, finned, and furred,

and who embraces each being
from the empowering surrender-stance
of the heart-warrior.

Beloved,

I'm wondering if you can hear
these words in the

wail of the full moon's light
or the song of the sky-breaching whale,

or the warble of the dawn-painting thrush,

or the woman-of-you who you
may still be denying knowing,

or the one whose voice you've heard
a thousand times,
but never really listened to,

or the one who you have yet to believe in
because you're still not fully
convinced that the Sacred Feminine
can show up in human form,

or that you are worthy of her affections.

My love,

I'm talking about
these words,
the ones that say with
open and iridescent sincerity:

"I am longing to receive you."

Should I repeat them?

These words:

"I am longing to receive you."

You see,

I know of the great aching
that stretches across this lush,
yet lamenting world of holy desire.

Can't you hear the evocative voices in the
swale of the moist wind and the
surge of the wave as it rises
and reaches out for something
to take hold of?

She wants you.

In the swaying of long meadow grasses,

in the rippling of the mountain stream
around an imperfect mossy stone,

in the releasing of perfume from every
splayed blossom,

she is speaking to you.

She wants you.

You see:

This poem...

This poem,
is an invitation that I have written
to the Sacred Masculine-of-you

It's an invitation to fully show up.
It's an invitation to be fully received.

It's an invitation to manifest,
in co-creative union,
embodied,
within me.

GIFTING YOU ROSES

I have twelve in my hand, yellow and tight.
On long stems, green and wildly-thorned.
I have captured the sun
and cast the warm glow of its light on memories
and truths and tomorrows.
Gratitude might be the answer to all of our questions.
I am grateful.
Do you know this day?
Do you know it, truly?
We cannot repeat miracles. What arrives,
arrives only once.
Do you see these petals?
Each is a never again, and I'm thankful for the opportunity
to trace the silken thread of their veins.
How can we not but look upon each as a miracle?
Yes, gratitude must be the answer to all our questions.
Today I have put my nose against
the window pane aside your front door.
I am carrying twelve yellow roses
because.
Yes,

because.

FIREFLIES

The dusks of humid summer days
have a magic about them
called fireflies.
Watch them blinking above the long grasses
and in the dark woodland.
Catch one, gently.
Hold it in the cup of your hand
and let it tickle walk across your
palm, all six legs striding, until it can't bear
the tangible for one second more and spreads its beetle
wings and becomes – how high can it go? – a star.

Now you are back in your childhood,
aren't you? And the glass jar is big
and has a metal lid. Probably, red.
It once held peanut butter,
and it makes a particular sound when you
open and close it. Do you hear it?

I remember what it felt like to spin the top on,
and spin the top off, and how you had
to be fast to get one in and not let the others out.

Back then,

did you ever imagine all the things that
a single jar could hold?

Mine has in it the voices of the other kids,
and their mothers calling them in.
Cars going down the street,

dogs barking,
lawn mowers falling silent for the night,

illusions that I thought were truths at the time.

And yellow – luminescent yellow.

"Come and be my lover," they said
"Go away! You scare me," they said.

I adored them and adore them still.

They taught me how to ask questions.
They taught me how to get silent enough to hear answers.

And,

they taught me how to be with things that go on in this world beyond our understanding.

How often the child of me
has saved the adult of me,
because she can remember fireflies.

ROBINS IN BLACK GUM

You can see how summer was good to them,
their robust breasts gleaming in the mirror of
the afternoon sun, and they are cheery. They
have a way of speaking about things that sounds
as if rejoicing, never reluctant, and this, even
after the early season freezes put ice on the pond
already. But they are meaningful too, dropping the
black gum seed where it will grow, and holly,
and I saw them not long ago at the dogwood berries.
Brilliant red. People don't think much about this
anymore, I know, but birds plant the forest. Other
animals do too. Squirrels, for sure. Yes, angels are
common among us and doing such good deeds. I
swear. How is it that we miss the grandeur of it all?

THE BERRIES

I could have picked
them. I didn't. Red.
Round. Winter saying
something, boldly.
Maybe to the red
bird in the green-
boughed pine. Maybe
to me. But, I have a
thought. It's about
beauty. Maybe it's a
test. The important
kind. Maybe someone
up there wants to
know if you can see
a thing and praise it
and that is all. This
I've tried. I can't do
it. Every time I walk
away, my heart is
full.

OUR FRIENDSHIP

What can I offer in reciprocity
but the spaciousness of
the "thank you"
that almost certainly
connects us in a million
different unifying ways.

The chord that was never
cut from my belly button
is the one that binds our
souls in a sweet firmament.

Friendship –

it is what births the
humanity in all of us.

Every time we come
full circle around the Sun,

We must ask ourselves,

am I yet born into the
family of all beings?

EVERY EVENING

I am like the mother who has never
had children, and so is mother to them all.

I cannot rest until they are where
their four legs should be at nightfall:

in the barn,
on the antiques and bookshelves,
boxes and baskets,
several on beds, one with a
head on my very own down pillow.

How could we settle for anything less than
a sacred ritual? "Are you safe?" We ask
the other.

And, we don't stop searching,

not
until we hear,

in some language,

"Yes."

MORNING RAIN

I am watching the mountains make clouds
out of the morning rain.
I am wondering what goes on inside a person
who can't come up with the word 'holy'
to describe this world.

I am contemplating savage beauty, and how
it cuts at the heart so that we might feel
into the fine texture of the fleshy body that conveys
us across this uneven ground for a short while.

Here, under these black walnut trees with
their damp-feathered pairs of indigo buntings,
the invisible hand of the Other lays firmly in the shallow cup
at the base of my back.

This is what it is like to wake up,
and greet another day.

SHORT POEM

        I'm going to tell you a secret:

        The holy is visible.

COMING HOME
to Earth and Cosmos

REASON ENOUGH

Today, I watched the sun wrap his long glowing fingers around a pine's narrow waist. It was a lover's embrace. I am sure of it. Daring things are happening – beautiful and fearless. I want to recognize them all. I want to tell about them. This would be reason enough to stay for a while longer. This is reason enough to have come at all.

JUST

Who says, "It is *just*?"

Oh, Lord. It has been me.

Is the dervish *just* whirling?
White skirts entrancing white roses
and also the white sun.

Is the witch hazel *just* blooming?
Golden, spidery blossoms,
and in Autumn for goodness sake!

Is the chestnut-sided warbler *just* here
and then gone? No! Think of it thundering
those tiny wings across the Americas.
Twice a year.
You can't do it. Not once. Nor can I.

Words can lead us to grace, and they can
call us away from the inherent sacred. "Don't look.
Something might change you."

OH!

I must stop.

This life is dedicated to Earth-praise,
to loving this unordinary world.

Words are my activism.
And, they are not *just* words.

THE SEED

If I am the embryo of the seed,
let me call this in which I am planted
my Mother's womb.

Here I am held.
Here I am nourished.
Here I am the possible human.

My umbilical cord is my root structure –
anchoring me to ancestral knowledge
and into the rich, organic detritus
of eroded lives
and savory fecal matter.

Everything that once was is a resource.

Everything.

Rain – the joy and grief of the world –
soaks and softens me.
Without it I become hardened, and
have no hope of intimacy with the light.

I must be cracked open to grow.

My limbs are the structures through which
my soul can reach, extending itself,
simultaneously longing to receive
and lamenting the ephemeral nature
of my gifts.

I show up because it's how I pray.
I unfurl because it's how I answer prayers.
I grow branches and leaves so that we have a place to meet.

I can bear flowers and fruit,
delicate, fragrant, and aphrodisiac sweet,
but not without having known relationship.

This is a place of co-creation.
Only the lonely believe in solitary forces
and the adversarial stance of their own mid-day shadow.

So, you see, these seeds of mySelf
that I place in your hands…

These are my way of saying, "I believe in you."

I'm asking you to do the next planting.

THE FIRST SOUNDS OF THE MORNING

What if you dedicated
the first sounds of the morning
to gratitude?

What then?

Might the birds, having just
limbered their wings and
stretched out the toes that
gripped all through the night,
comment on
your voice at dawn?

Might the trees who have
known so little appreciation for
their shade and fruits,
cry,

like lovers cry when the
moment they never believed
would come
is suddenly a memory?

Might the sun, a
Master of Power,
finally learn what it
feels like to receive warmth?

I've heard the jack-in-the-pulpit
silently rendering a sermon,

and watched a muskrat put his

hands in prayer position
just before nibbling off golden
flower heads

as dawn pinked.

I'm thinking that it would be good
to realize that we are Home
every morning,

and to give thanks for the
privilege.

CATERPILLARS

All summer long they are out there chewing
on something that is unable to shoo away their
multitude of tiny, suckered feet.

Maybe it calls out to the birds,

"Come! Perch here! Eat these!"

And, some birds do, definitely,
and toads,
and mantises,
wasps with effective yet questionable tactics, those
ladybird beetles that you naively think
so lovely and kind,

but there are still more
scissoring away at the edges, sculpting, stripping,
all feeling fully entitled to gluttony;
there will be no acknowledgement of sin, oh no,
no repenting, no statements of any kind that
end with

Amen.

I love them.

Every single one is perfect in its beingness,
and I needn't struggle with the ethics of it all.

~

I listened to the evening news.

How much longer until the butterflies emerge?

I'm not sure that I have the patience to wait.

NUTHATCH LOGIC

Today, in the wood, I decided to converse with nuthatch. "Nuthatch," I said, "the world seems upside down."

And, nuthatch squeaked in the way nuthatches do, and replied:

"I can see how you would see it that way. I don't understand how you people get around the way you do,

all that blood going to your feet. It must be hard to think."

And, I could say no more.

THE RHYTHM

We've all heard
our mother's heart beat
from beneath her skin.

This is our rhythm –
an inherited sense
of right and righteous timing.

"Home" and "Not Home"
are sequences, patterns,
familiar and unfamiliar.

All your life,
memory has been
the drummer –
and you've marched.

Has it served you well –
This rhythm?
This onward march?

Recently, I've been lying
on the Earth in fetal position –

and listening.

This is when I really re-
member
that sound, this feeling.

This is when I re-member the
ancient rhythms of
The Mother.

This is when I know
I no longer need to
march.

This is when I know
I'm home –

Everywhere,
and always.

The first mother
would have embodied
this rhythm.

Somewhere down the line
someone missed
a beat,

and we've all been missing
it ever since.

So profoundly missing it.

Now.

Head upon the heart.

It's up to us to re-member.

Head upon the heart?

Cheek on bark or moss or stone.

Are you listening?

This is what the future
will hear.

WHO PAINTS THE SKY

    Who paints the sky? And, why has it
taken me so long to think to ask?
I want to know who is up there
to love, and how I can bargain, if
I might, for more days to end like
this one:
in attentiveness,
in wonderment,
in devotion.

GINSENG THIEVES

I found them on knee, on a Saturday morning,
digging three-pronged ginseng.

I told them to stop. And, go. And, was
only semi-polite about it.

They seemed surprised that I could arrive
there, just then, and spot
them in their leafy camo, such baggy pants,

and that I could speak a thing or two about the blond
roots (they'd broken most of the root hairs) gripped in
their pocket-buried hands, to which
red clay still clung, hopeful, that I'd get it set back
within this earth;

It still had work to do:

This world needs holding.

~

This is what it is like to suddenly
realize that you are inhabiting
your belonging:

The forest had called out
to me by a name

I knew.

THE NATURE OF COOPERATION

They had barely opened their eyes
when the darkness came, muscular and slithering,
forked-tongue tasting the air, lapping
his way through the round portal to the other world –
a world they were yet to hear the stories of –

They had no need. Everything had come to them.
And, this was coming too.

Yes, well. Truth be told, I wasn't there.

But I know.

I know because we met in the barn only moments
passed and he was bulging with what I had
only yesterday decided to love.

I sighed, and decided to love equally,

but continued to wonder on this mysterious
planet for a bit – its gives and takes.

Who wins? Who loses?

I was taught to ask that question.
It's typically a force of nature to act against
each other they'd said.

Predation. Competition. Parasitism.

I opened the wooden box and looked inside.
Empty.

But it's early yet, perhaps, they'll try again,
I mused.

Honestly, I hoped.

Then the big questions alighted:

Could this loss have been an act of
greater-than-self service – a death for
something else to live by?

What does it look like to feed the holy?

An ill-missioned chickadee perched on
the nearest fence post, a small green caterpillar
in its dainty, sharp beak.

I wonder if we are so closed off to
the concept of cooperation,

to faith in cooperation,

that we so seldom see it nested in the relationships
being enacted around us,

so rarely choose to speak that word, with its plentitude
of circular lettering.

But the soul knows:

Everything depends on the body of otherness.
I have to believe

we have somehow forgotten a sacred agreement
that we once said "yes" to in the company of wild things.
And, at the very least,
most certainly at the very least,

I believe,
We should be offering thanks.
In abundance.

THESE BONES

It seems that I am forever
trying to fall in love with
these bones, and the flesh
that keeps them hidden
away so that they might remain
mostly unspeakable.

This is your story too, if you are
honest about it. Being human.

~

When I was a little girl, my mother dressed
me in brightly colored bathing suits so that
I could be spotted way down the beach;
even then, I had a penchant for wandering.

I bent over sand buckets to identify shells for
delighted old ladies and gentleman, handed
sharks' teeth to astonished little boys,
but gathered the round, white vertebrae of
ocean-going fish for myself; a wild child seeks
adornment from the sea.

All you need is some string and you
can make a necklace.

And, there have been other bones:

Turtles left to the elements at roadside,
the deer the hunters lost to forest secrets,
dogs piled high at the end of an old road in

the middle of nowhere on a day that I had dedicated
to being charmed by birdsong and birds,

and I have visited museums, many of them,
where bones stare back at you, begging you to
remember a life that you never knew, to
imagine something when it was ensouled
and might have chosen to eat you for being so
close, or it might have run. But, it wouldn't
have stayed, not like this. Not this still, forever.

These other things are so easy to love, like this
stark day with the sycamores bearing their ribs.

~

They say that poems should have good bones.
Stories can be ligaments and tendons.

~

I wonder what our Mother feels in that moment
when we walk away from her for the very
first time,

and later when she hears us remark:

"I have been abandoned."

How easily we abandon ourselves
to stories in which we do not belong.

~

Here, on Earth, we live such a story.
Being human.

~

I love all the old stories – the ancient ones –
in which ancestors are more than just bones,

just bones,

especially when the ancestors were not
just human like they are now,

in our way of speaking of

the world as not needing us.

~

Maybe, someone will adorn
themselves with these bones,
my bones.

It could, perhaps,
be me.

THE SNAKE

> Judge me to be a vile trickster, a low
> life. Project all your fears onto me.
> These things, I can shed.
>
> Accept my invitation to place the belly
> of your entire being on the skin of
> the Earth, to undulate, sensuously,
> across the terrain of the divine feminine,
> to understand this place, your place,
> our place.
>
> There is a gateway to heaven.

YOU MUST BREATHE

When there is thick, soft silt below your feet
and water
dense and long overhead,
re-member that you must breathe.

You must fill your lungs.

You must rise, at some point,
and breathe.

This being human requires
that we let something
of this world
in.

SAYING GOODBYE

I stood there in the thick, milky dusk,
my boots bedded in rotting straw and the withered
bodies of plants that I had dug into this place.
We tended each other for a season.
I knew them by touch and smell,
and how slight variations in color or a pucker
of leaf were words wanting understanding.
I came here to learn to listen.
The tomato hornworm caterpillars visited,
and the cabbage butterflies,
and we shared,
time and other things.
Wings. I've always wanted a pair, or two.
When I was on my knees,
I wondered who had stripped this land raw,
and why so much of this practice
was new to me at this age,
and what the earthworms thought
about while navigating
the valleys and ridges of my rough palms.
Could they tell how much I adored them?
Oh, yes, these were the musings of summer,
thoughts freed while the mind
had the luxury of abundance.
This though was Autumn. It was Autumn waning:
As I looked into the night to come,
I saw a cricket lying down,
frost crystals colonizing his legs.
Goodbyes needed to be said.
A garden can teach us to be earnest with this word,
Goodbye.
At the interface of starvation
and nourishment is where to harvest

the roots of deep gratitude.
And so, I began to offer this word to the yet-living,
letting the growing sense of emptiness
be my understanding.
"Goodbye."
"Goodbye."
And again,
"Goodbye."
Inside,
the woodstove was awaiting me.

ROSES ARE OUT OF SEASON

Sometimes the beloved
is a place
that chooses you
in your sleep
while you are busily dreaming
of a human form that hasn't yet
crossed the threshold of your
weary front door.

How bittersweet the sip of tonic
when you realize that
the reclining land on which
you've been walking barefoot,
while casting your laments like seed, has
been – all the while – caressing your
filthy, calloused feet,

That the dawns that you casually inhale
with your first morning breath have been
the red lips of the horizon

starting your day with a wide-reaching kiss, and

that the feeling of being unable to move,
what you've fought like a panicked person
in a pool of quickening sand,
was really the sensation of being held in a
long, conditionless embrace.

I've seen this: how some people
can't get away – how they eventually
surrender in love, or misery.

The one who calls you home
has many faces,

Today, I recognize him in yellowed
walnut leaves
falling on the path ahead of me.

Roses are out of season.

IT IS THROUGH YOU

You are not apart from Her,
but a part of Her.

It is through your eyes that Her beauty
gains form and story,
and too that heart-wrenching lament
that initiates boys into authentic manhood.

It is through your ears that Her song
finds the drum and rhythm,
and too that ancient requiem of longing
that Sees the wild yearning to be
seen in the woman who has not fully
forgotten what a humming child
knows of liberation.

Through your calloused hands,
She touches her own body.

Through your bare and wanting feet,
She can travel to places of Herself
in the way that
none of us can go alone.

So, this I must say:
Take no part in your tale of unworthiness.
Make short banter with all language of doubt.
Let there be no more epic sagas in which the hero
falls silently upon the very sword that She
has forged for him of Her very own
smelted heart.

No Sir.

As a part of Her myself and upon Her behalf
in the manner that serves all kin
baring close resemblance to the
Breath of Life,

I ask of you this with a polite
yet rabid fierceness, because anything else
would be too small an effort in lieu of
what is most important,

Do this:

Upon every tender inspiration,
Upon every harrowed vulnerability,
let your tongue drip
with languid bliss and humor
the wisest of trembling pearls –

all the while knowing,

you speak,

with the Mother's tongue.

THE ROOTS

There's a little boy that I've been watching,
all dressed in white linen,
on his knees,
digging,
desperately seeking The Roots.

He's finally found them,
fingers raw and blooded by perseverance,
but there they are -

long residing at the base of
Rumi's lamenting reed.

Cut off from our ancient lineage
we cannot but cry out
for a vision of Home –

Though the meaning of the
deep inner wailing may
elude us for many generations,

And the masks we take up
make us unrecognizable even
in our own mirrors,

We cannot deny the sound
emanating from our own
severed soul.

It's the one that constantly
tells us that we don't belong here,

that we have been forsaken,

and that we have forsook.

Rumi's reed longed for a heart
so that it could explain
the pain of its yearning
to return to its roots.

This I have.

And so let me tell you how
I have ached:

Like the fledgling thrown
from the nest,
thinking its tending parents
now want it destroyed
on the hard ground below.

Like the Autumn leaves
torn away by winds before
they had conversed
long enough to learn the
names of all the other leaves
on all the other branches.

Like the rock rolled down
the mountain slope
in the wash of heavy winter rains,

never again to know the
boulder in which it was
brought forth from the belly well
of the inner Earth.

This is the power of Love,
I am told:

To dare to risk your offspring
so that they may learn to fly.

To make offerings of yourself
to the Holy that nourishes
you from above and below.

To surrender to the pull of gravity
as a humble act of coming
onto the knees of all Creation.

To dig until the melancholy fingers yield
the droplets of bloodlines
that have departed across entire
Oceans of destiny.

I am the last.

The last child has been taken
from me by the jealous hunters,
and so it stops with me.

I am the last.

I am the last to be the cut reed
and the reed cutter,

The oppressed
and the oppressor.

I am the last to forsake
the Truth
and be forsaken by
the story my lineage
construed to keep us
women safe.

Now is the time that
we must return to our
power,

That we must reclaim
the connection to our Earth-deep
roots and grow forth
again with a ripeness
that when savored
seeks only to unite.

But how?

Acknowledgment.

Acknowledging the suffering
of every reed cut
and of every reed cutter
who has been chased by
the fear of his own death.

Honoring.

Honoring the fleshy sacrifice of the reed
and the soul loss of the
reed cutter,

and the gift of shelter that they
somehow managed to
co-creatively manifest.

Learning.

Learning to hear the reed's
cry in my own voice,
and yours,
and too in the voice of the
reed cutters within.

Learning that the sound
most needed now is one
of joy.

Re-membering.

Re-membering how to find
the way back to the Earth
through dark passageways,
carrying with me every
incense-infused gift
that my ancestors have passed down
in the wrappings of the prayers that
someday,
this day,

I would take up
the alchemical bundle
called Love
and return with it to my roots.

And so I anoint that little boy
and his Mother
with the purest essence of belonging,
praying that they will no longer
feel disconnected, lonely, and unloved.

And down the matrilineal line
this too I receive.

The hungry ghosts will find that there
is nothing left here on which
to feed;

I can again draw nourishment
from who I am.

I am the black bird with a heart
who remembers the holy song
of the forgiving flute
made out of sacred reed.

AT THE TURN OF THE DAY

At the turn of the day you must agree to one thing:
To love this world more than you fear it.
Go forward with your disappointments. Watch
how even the light chooses a place to die, beautifully. We
can never know what becomes of unutterable
questions, or why we were made for this particular life and
not another.
I find it useful to be delighted:
something just happened that I can't explain.

ACKNOWLEDGMENTS

Many thanks to Jason Kirkey for designing the cover and laying out the text. A deep bow to all of you who have welcomed my poems into your lives. Your presence is muse.

We're all just walking each other home.
—RAM DASS

ABOUT THE AUTHOR

Jamie K. Reaser has a passion for bringing people into their hearts, inspiring the heartbeat of community, and, ultimately, empowering people to live with a heart-felt dedication to Mother Earth. Her award-winning writing explores the inter-relatedness of Nature and human nature. Jamie's collections of poetry include, *Huntley Meadows: A Naturalist's Journal in Verse*, *Note to Self: Poems for Changing the World from the Inside Out*, *Sacred Reciprocity: Courting the Beloved in Everyday Life*, *Wild Life: New* and *Selected Poems*, and *Winter: Reflections by Snowlight*. She is a Fellow of the International League of Conservation Writers.

Jamie makes her home at Ravens Ridge Farm in the Blue Ridge Mountains of Virginia.

Selected poems are can be found on the Talking Waters poetry blog at http://www.talkingwaters-poetry.blogspot.com, or through Talking Waters on Facebook.

CPSIA information can be obtained
at www.ICGtesting.com
Printed in the USA
LVHW092337200120
644179LV00003B/427